MW01610484

Antarctica

Leila Merrell Foster

Heinemann Library
Chicago, Illinois

Designed by Depke Design
Printed in Hong Kong

05 04 03 02
10 9 8 7 6 5 4 3 2

Library of Congress Cataloging-in-Publication Data
Foster, Leila Merrell.
  Antarctica / Leila Merrell Foster.
     p. cm. -- (Continents)
Includes bibliographical references.
  ISBN 1-57572-447-2 (lib. bdg.)   ISBN 1-58810-946-1 (pbk. bdg.)
  1. Antarctica--Juvenile literature. 2. Ecology--Antarctica--Juvenile
literature. [1. Antarctica.] I. Title. II. Continents (Chicago, Ill.)
  G863 .F67 2001
  919.8'9--dc21   00-011465

Acknowledgments
The publishers are grateful to the following for permission to reproduce copyright material:
Tony Stone/Ben Osborne, p. 4; Earth Scenes/David C. Fritts, p. 6; Tony Stone/Kim Heacox, p. 7; Peter Arnold/Gordon Wiltsie, pp. 8, 13; Tony Stone/Kim Westerskov, pp. 11, 17, 28; Photo Edit/Anna Zuckermann, p. 15; Photo Edit/Jack S. Grove, p. 16; Bruce Coleman/Fritz Polking, Inc., p. 20; Animals Animals/Johnny Johnson, p. 21; Earth Scenes/Stefano Nicolini, p. 22; Earth Scenes/Patti Murray, p. 23; Corbis/Bettmann Archive, p. 24; The Granger Collection, p. 25; Peter Arnold/Bruno P. Zehnder, p. 27; Earth Scenes/B. Herrod, p. 29.

Every effort has been made to contact copyright holders of any material reproduced in this book. Any omissions will be rectified in subsequent printings if notice is given to the publisher.

Some words are shown in bold, **like this.**
You can find out what they mean by looking
in the glossary.

Contents

Where Is Antarctica?

Mountains in Antarctica

There are seven continents in the world. Antarctica is the fifth largest. It surrounds the **South Pole.** It is shaped almost like a circle. A strip of land sticks out toward South America.

Antarctica is the coldest and iciest continent. It is far from the **equator.** The coldest temperature ever recorded was in Antarctica in 1983.

Ice Sheet

Transantarctic Mountains

Almost all of Antarctica is buried under a thick layer of ice and snow. This layer is called the Antarctic **ice sheet**.

Tabular iceberg, Wedell Sea

The Antarctic ice sheet has more **freshwater** than any other area on Earth. If the ice sheet melted, cities on **coasts** around the world would be flooded.

South Pole

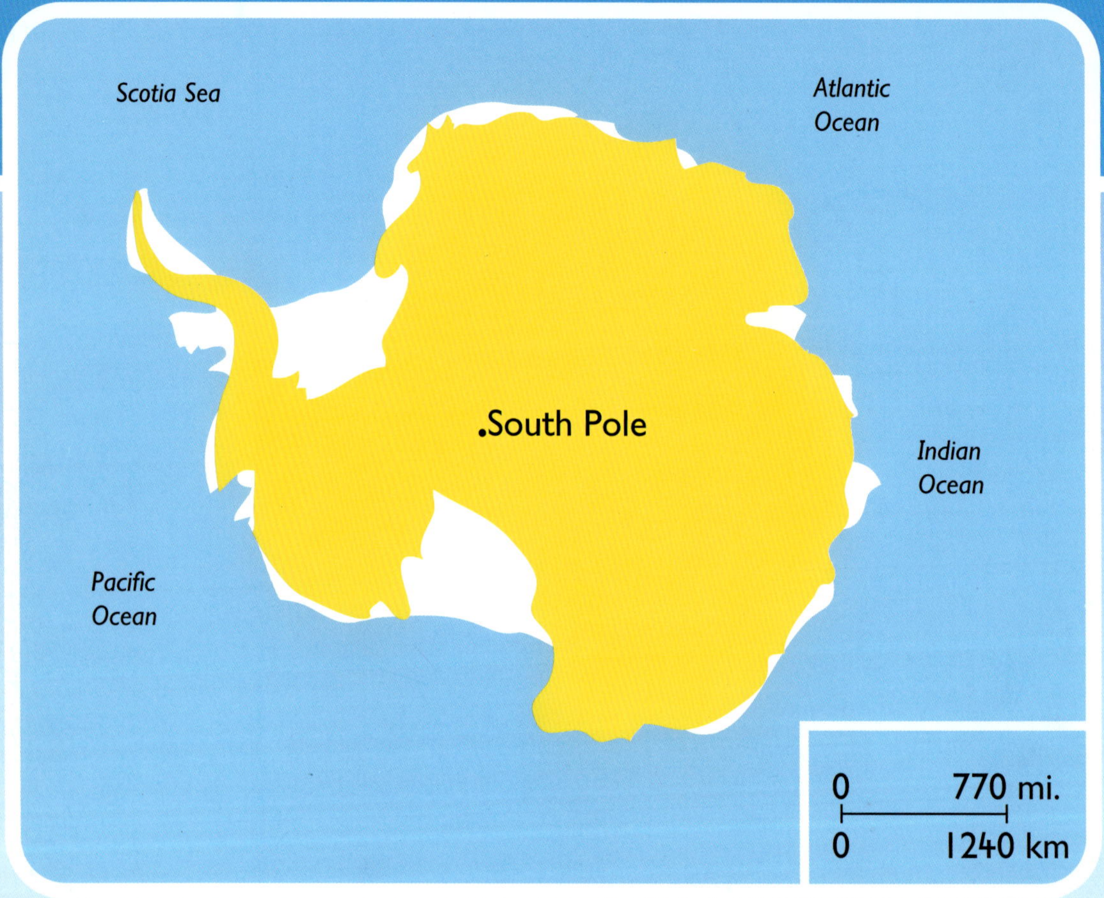

Scotia Sea

Atlantic Ocean

.South Pole

Indian Ocean

Pacific Ocean

0	770 mi.
0	1240 km

The **South Pole** is the most famous place in Antarctica. The south pole and the north pole are the points around which Earth spins.

Geographic South Pole

People have set up a real pole at the South Pole.
A person can easily walk around the world there.
If the **ice sheet** in which the pole is set moves,
then the pole has to be moved, too.

Weather

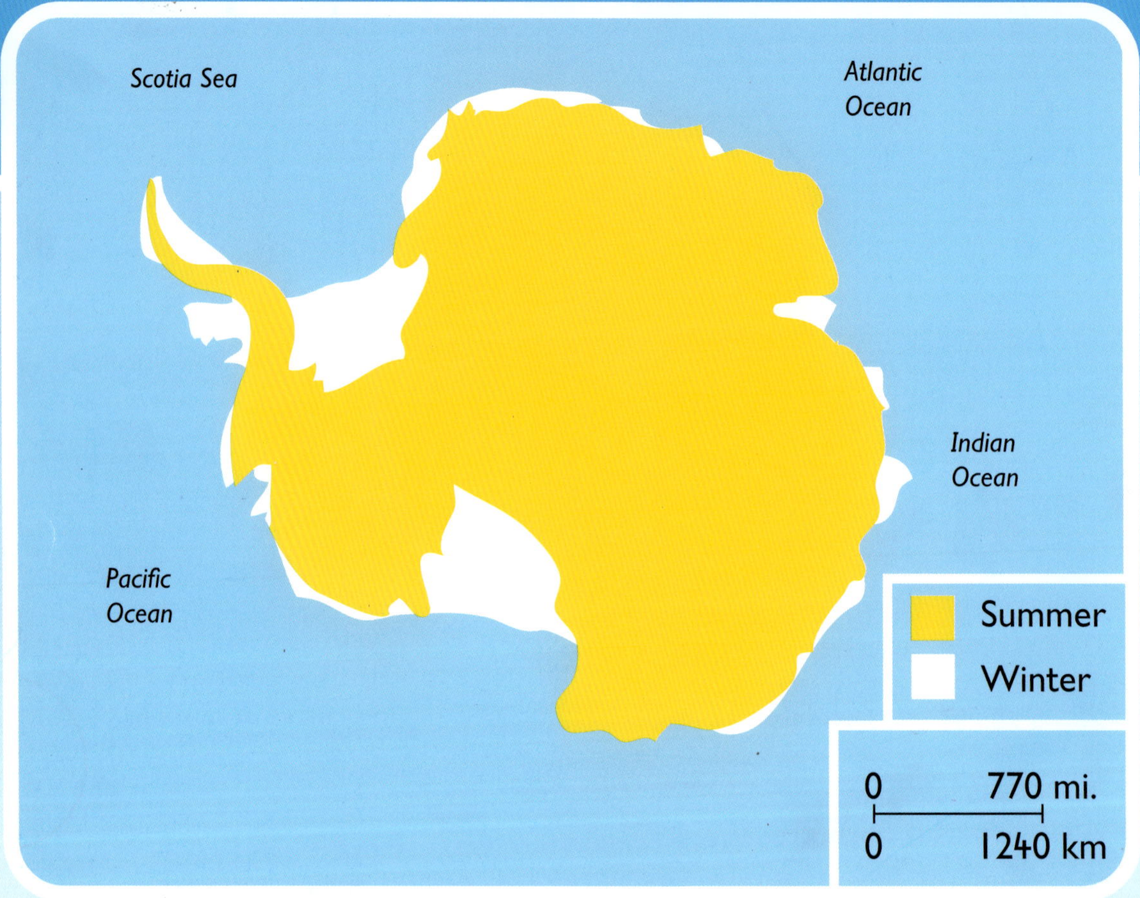

Scotia Sea

Atlantic Ocean

Indian Ocean

Pacific Ocean

Summer
Winter

0	770 mi.
0	1240 km

In the winter, Antarctica gets twice as big. Ocean water around the continent freezes. The Atlantic, Pacific, and Indian Oceans surround the continent.

Middle Antarctica

The middle of Antarctica is a desert. Very little snow or rain falls there. Wind whips up blizzards from the snow already on the ground. Rain and snow fall along the **coasts.**

Mountains

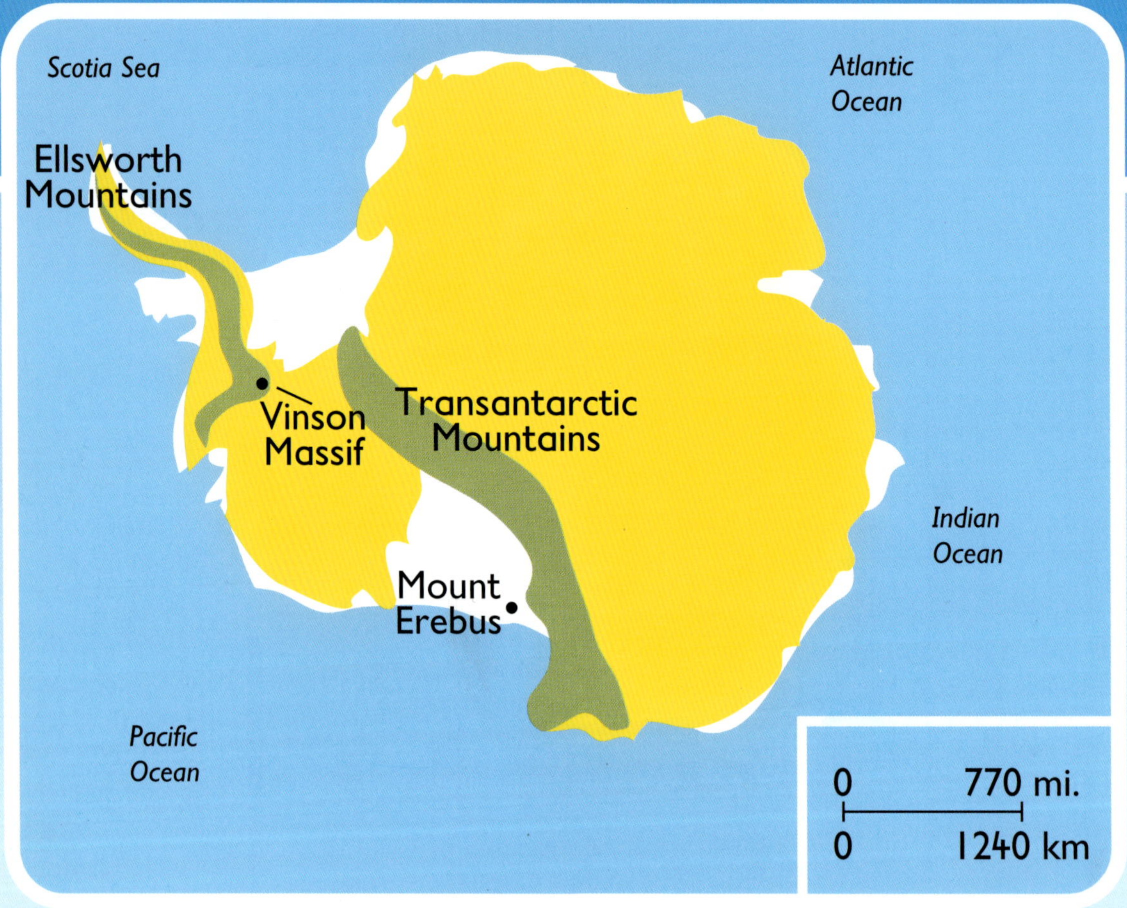

Scotia Sea

Atlantic Ocean

Ellsworth Mountains

Vinson Massif

Transantarctic Mountains

Indian Ocean

Mount Erebus

Pacific Ocean

| 0 | 770 mi. |
| 0 | 1240 km |

The Transantarctic Mountains divide East and West Antarctica. Nearby Mount Erebus is an active volcano.

Vinson Massif, Ellsworth Mountains

The highest point on the continent is the Vinson **Massif.** It is in the Ellsworth Mountains in western Antarctica.

Ice

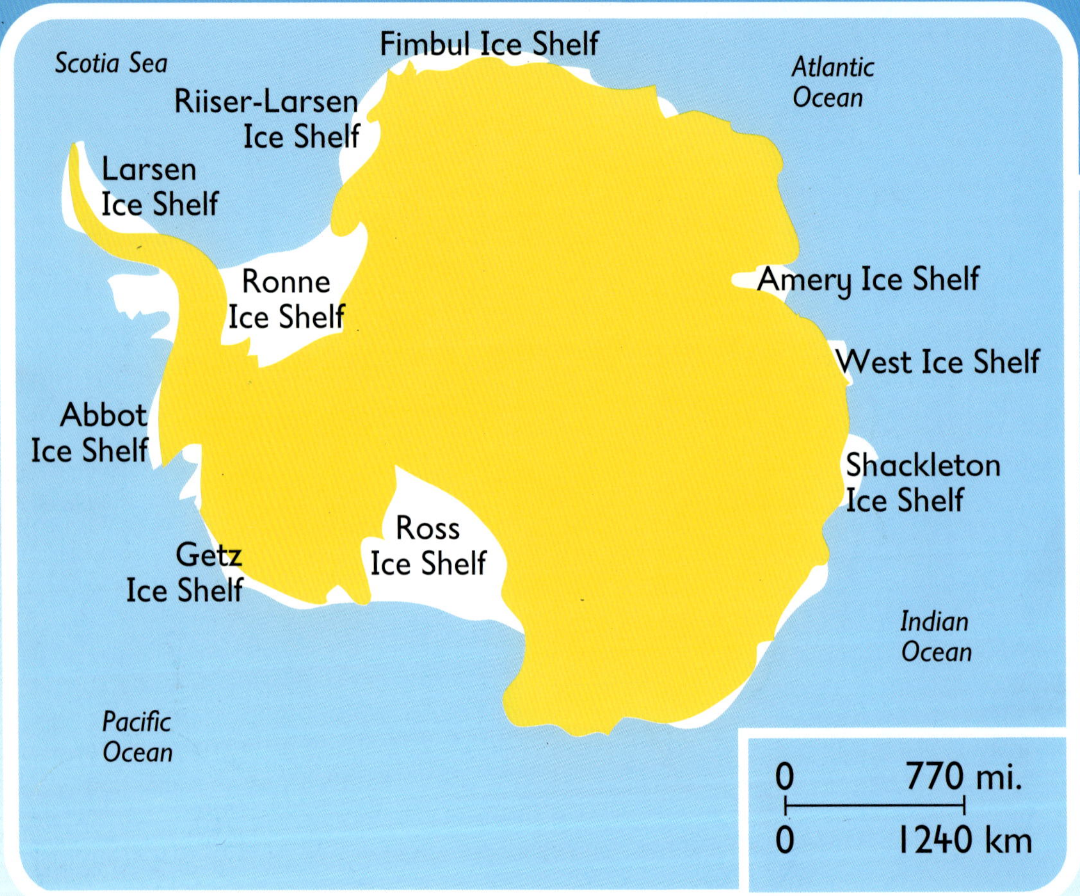

Scotia Sea

Fimbul Ice Shelf

Riiser-Larsen
Ice Shelf

Atlantic
Ocean

Larsen
Ice Shelf

Ronne
Ice Shelf

Amery Ice Shelf

West Ice Shelf

Abbot
Ice Shelf

Shackleton
Ice Shelf

Getz
Ice Shelf

Ross
Ice Shelf

Indian
Ocean

Pacific
Ocean

0	770 mi.
0	1240 km

Huge mountains of ice hang over the sea like shelves. The Ross **Ice Shelf** is the largest. It is the size of the state of Texas.

Iceberg near Elephant Island, Antarctica

Icebergs are formed when ice breaks off and floats free. Most of the world's icebergs float around Antarctica. They are also the largest icebergs in the world.

 Glaciers

![Mertz Glacier photograph]

Mertz Glacier

Glaciers are large bodies of ice and snow.
Glaciers in Antarctica are slowly moving from
the center of the continent to the edges. The
snow is so clean that people can melt it to drink.

Glacier

You can't see glaciers move because they move very slowly—but they do move! The ice at the bottom of the glacier gets squashed by the ice above. The whole glacier then slides along.

# Oceans and Seas

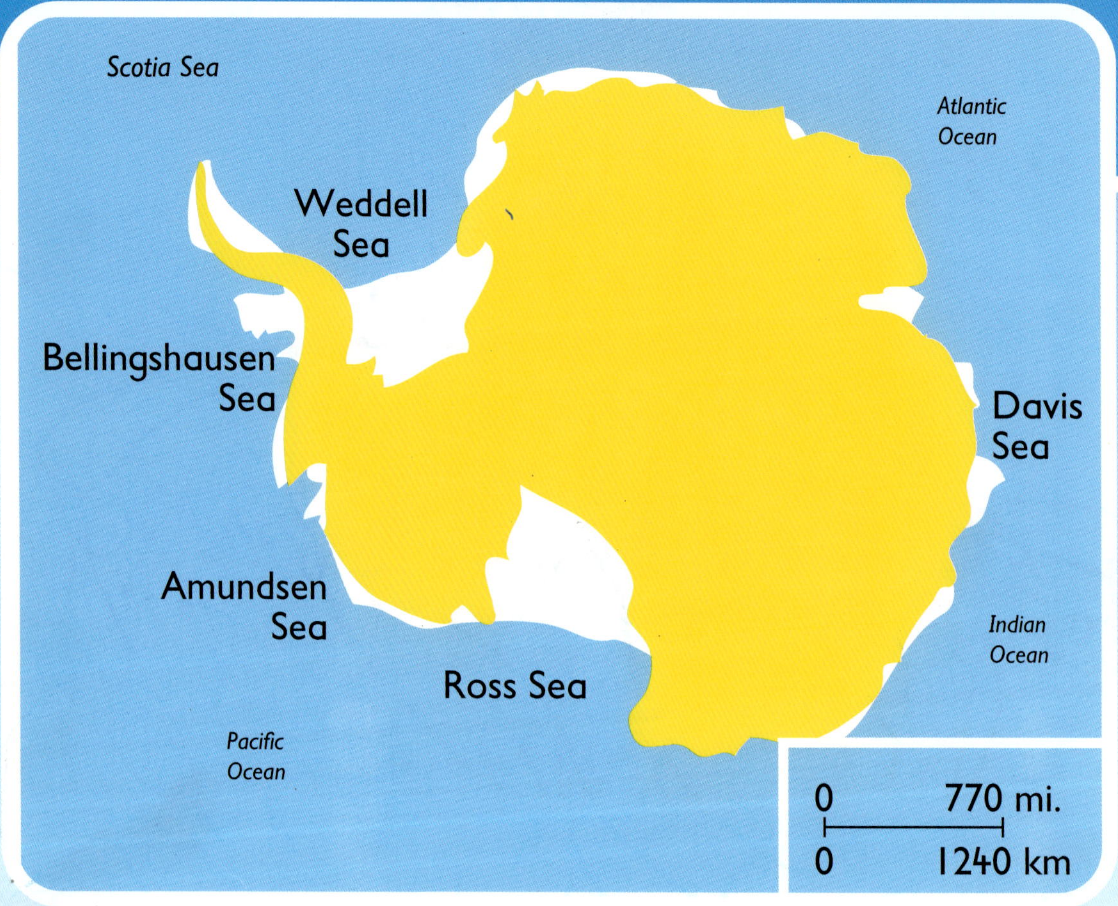

Scotia Sea

Atlantic
Ocean

Weddell
Sea

Bellingshausen
Sea

Davis
Sea

Amundsen
Sea

Indian
Ocean

Ross Sea

Pacific
Ocean

0	770 mi.
0	1240 km

The waters around Antarctica circle the
continent in a westerly direction. The cold
waters of the southern oceans stop the **icebergs**
from melting quickly.

Storm near iceberg

Sea water near the **coasts** also protects Antarctica's ice. This cold water stops warmer water from the Atlantic, Pacific, and Indian Oceans from reaching and melting the ice.

Animals

Emperor penguins

About 45 kinds of birds live on Antarctica. Most of these birds fly north for the winter months. The emperor penguin stays. It is one kind of penguin that **breeds** there.

Elephant seals

In the past, people hunted the whales and seals that lived in and near Antarctica. Now there are laws that protect these animals from hunters.

Plants

![Lichen, Penguin Island, Antarctica]

Lichen, Penguin Island, Antarctica

Lichen is the most common plant that grows in Antarctica. It grows like moss on rocks and is bright orange and yellow. Few plants can live in the icy, cold **climate** of Antarctica.

Tussock grass, Sea Lion Island, Antarctica

The only grass that grows on Antarctica is called tussock. It grows in the areas farthest north, where it is the warmest.

Explorers

Endurance trapped in ice

People tried to explore Antarctica by sailing in wooden ships. Strong, sharp ice easily tore apart their boats. Today, special ice-breaking ships take people to Antarctica.

Roald Amundsen

The first person to reach the **South Pole** was Roald Amundsen in 1911. He used dog sleds. Today, airplanes make the trip easier.

 # All the Countries

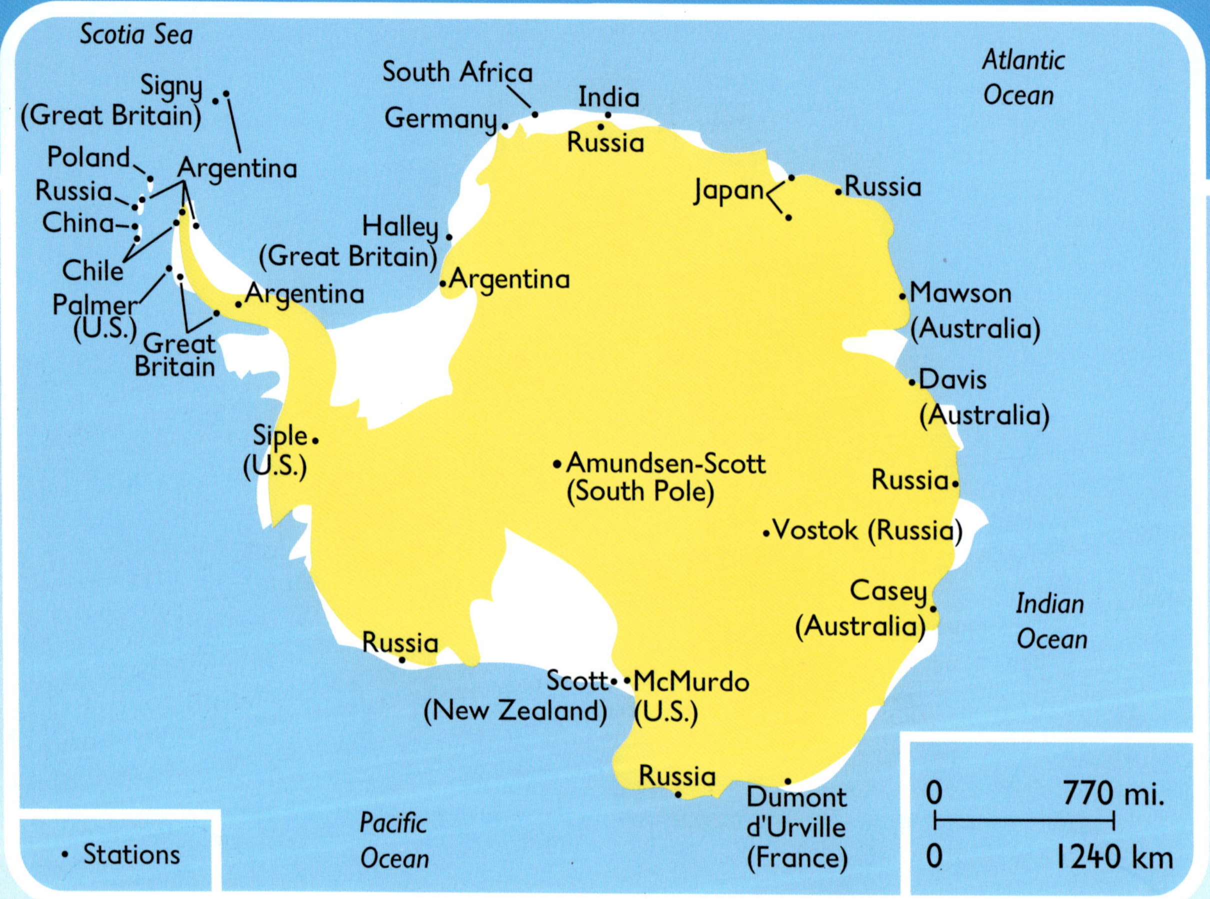

Scotia Sea

Signy
(Great Britain)

South Africa

Germany

India

Russia

Atlantic
Ocean

Poland

Russia

China

Argentina

Japan

Russia

Chile

Halley
(Great Britain)

Palmer
(U.S.)

Argentina

Argentina

Mawson
(Australia)

Great
Britain

Davis
(Australia)

Siple
(U.S.)

Amundsen-Scott
(South Pole)

Russia

Vostok (Russia)

Casey
(Australia)

Indian
Ocean

Russia

Scott
(New Zealand)

McMurdo
(U.S.)

• Stations

Russia

Pacific
Ocean

Dumont
d'Urville
(France)

0	770 mi.
0	1240 km

There are no countries in Antarctica. Many countries from other continents have **stations** in Antarctica. Scientists work and do experiments there.

McMurdo Station

Those countries and others have agreed to keep Antarctica open to everyone. Scientists and **tourists** from every country in the world can work or visit there.

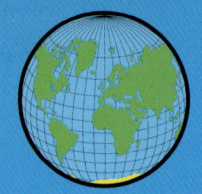

Science

![McMurdo Station]

McMurdo Station

Scientists study the stars in the long, dark winter months. Others test and do experiments on the **atmosphere** above Antarctica.

Berkner Island, Antarctica

Scientists drill holes in the ice to learn about the **climate.** Others study the rocks to find out how old they are and what they are made of.

Fast Facts

1. Antarctica's thickest ice is more than 15,000 feet (4,800 meters)—almost 5 miles!

2. The coldest temperature ever recorded was at Vostok Station on July 21, 1983. It was −128.6° F (−89.2° C).

3. The island plateau of Antarctica receives no rain. It has one of the driest climates on Earth.

4. Scientists have found fossils in Antarctica. This means that the continent was once warm and that trees and other plants lived there.

5. Antarctica is dark for four months each year.

6. Only a few insects and other tiny animals spend their entire lives on Antarctica.

Glossary

active volcano hole in the earth from which hot, melted rock is thrown out

atmosphere air surrounding the earth

breed to have babies

climate kind of weather a place has

coast land right next to water

equator imaginary circle around the exact middle of the earth

fossil remains or imprint in stone of a plant or animal

freshwater water that is not salty

glacier very large mass of slow-moving ice and snow

iceberg large piece of ice that is floating in the sea

ice sheet very thick covering of ice that covers a large area of land, also called an ice cap

ice shelf ice that extends from land over water

massif another word for a mountain

plateau area of high, flat land

South Pole most southern spot on the earth, around which the earth spins

station place for scientists to work

tourist person visiting a place for fun

More Books to Read

Stone, Lynn M. *The Antarctic.* Vero Beach, Fla.: Rourke Publishing Group, 1996.

Stone, Lynn M. *Life in the Antarctic.* Vero Beach, Fla.: Rourke Publishing Group, 1995.

Wheeler, Sara. *Greetings from Antarctica.* Lincolnwood, Ill.: NTC Contemporary Publishing Co., 1999.

Index